After the Formalities

Anthony Anaxagorou

Penned in the Margins

LONDON

PUBLISHED BY PENNED IN THE MARGINS
Toynbee Studios, 28 Commercial Street, London E1 6AB
www.pennedinthemargins.co.uk

First published 2019

Printed in the United Kingdom by CPI Group (UK) Ltd

ISBN
978-1-908058-65-2

CONTENTS

THANKS

To Sabrina Mahfouz, Joelle Taylor, Jack Underwood, Wayne Holloway-Smith and Chimene Suleyman: thank you for trusting these poems and for your generous instruction. Thank you to Arts Council England. To Tom MacAndrew and Sarah Sanders.

To my agent Claudia Young at Greene & Heaton and to Tom Chivers at Penned in the Margins. Thank you for believing in the work. To my family. To my friends. To the wonderful poets of today who continue to make extraordinary and vital work during these fractious times.

To my beloved grandmother who passed away during the writing of this book. I miss you very much. And to my son, Tabari: I hope when I'm old you'll read these poems with the same fondness I discovered when writing them.

In memory of Stella Stylianou

January 1922 – January 2018

After the Formalities

The voice is a second face

GÉRARD BAUËR

Lockstep

to those

        fathers

        their boys

the way it has to happen

Cause

& to the burning I say
　　my worry is a whole country.

I've been myself longer
than my undoing —
　　　　heavy trunk of silverware
museum glass polish
　　　　portraiture
of bent flags.

I'm here as my grandparents were
　　　　only with a moving mouth.

　　During empire
my people were subjects first
citizens later　　once the vigilantes
managed to zip up their coats

　　　flames lambent

my grandmother died with umbrellas
outstretched in her gut my grandmother
   died

    to be British
 is to be everywhere.

     Some roots
have been in the earth
   for so long
they know only to call themselves earth.

A worm's pink nipple bleeds into snow.

  My birth
my mother's brown skin I'd already
filled half myself with Britannia's
air it took them a month to find my name.

Departure Lounge Twenty Seventeen

Before Trump marshalled January
to do winter's work to breach fruit

    children peppered oceans
    like ends of warm bread

before Harvey Weinstein Tarana Burke
spoke smoke into a litany of nuns

    before functionaries filled death ledgers
    with names they mispronounced

before Theresa May triggered Article 50
crouched on a wet rooftop in Lisbon

    the departure lounge was heavy
    with pilots who no longer trusted the sky

& my grandmother is making her way
into a forest barefoot

before floral tributes crown
a Mancunian grief

    before *Celotex* expressed sympathies
    for the seventy-two it turned into moons

& my grandmother is making her way
into a forest barefoot

    before oceans reversed slowly into cages
    like blue meat in a slaughterhouse

before the Pope prayed in apology
for the drift of the refugee crunching roaches

    underfoot before Darren Osborne sat in a room
    full of his mood watching *Three Girls* too loud

I wished to god
I could keep my wishing for my son

    but before I turn I need to leave
    the rubbish where it can be seen:

a mountain has abandoned snow
freezing hands to warn my heart

    & no matter how many times I try forgetting
    I still hear

my grandmother's name yelled into a forest
its bodies taking on water

    chainsaws stressing honey at the root
    I'm calling

but January keeps my voice for itself
dumping it where only wilderness breeds

    lifting memory   spilling into cloud
before washing her feet   before clipping her nails
    before watching her turn to face the gone

Four Small Indiscretions

We came from the south, spun from forty sperm
                blaming the Achaeans or the scimitar

my grandmother's suitcase was three-part crucifix
                one-part donkey dung

it's worth noting
                beyond Socratic thought, Mount Elbrus,
                the Knights Hospitaller and their
                arquebuses

how throughout school I believed the British proof
                stored in my vault, coral fructifying
                manacles

spent my strangest coins on their thickest books
                only to keep finding myself a murmur

it's also worth noting the 1960 Treaty of Guarantee, Cyprus
                and my father's reluctance to confess

at the age of three teachers branded me a mute

                            words were just odd signs with tiny legs.

This week I've had eight rejections

                     leaving me feeling like a breatharian

stepping out a Bronze Age bath,

                 Cleitus watching Alexander pour his last,

                 the sun setting, Europa feeding Zeus a sick

                 fowl.

Like most Westerners when I find myself lost

                 I venture Eastwards with nothing

but a gaze and an idea

                 I never make it past airport security

who question where I'm headed and why;

                 each night my son sketches my face

with his strongest lines and the last of his reds,

                 for him it's always the beginning

I tuck each drawing between a book so in years to come
                    when he wants to know and people

stop to ask if it's true
                    he can smile before saying, of course.

Uber

door
shuts
winds slap
a *Magic Tree*
around a
radio hums
songs
into us both
one of two
phones
rings
from an edge
he tells her
he'll call back
in a language
half
packed
back
when
I assume

things
took a turn
for the worse
a flag
hanging
from the rear
view
I ask where
he says
Mauritius
returning
my question
I say
Cyprus
asking
if he prefers
it here
he says
sleep
is easier
the roads
at night
less congested

at the lights
I ask about
children
from his
pocket
he pulls
a photo
of a girl
I note
the way
her smile
matches
her mother's
in the picture
everyone's
together
smiling
she turned
nine last
week
he said
it's been
over five

years
now
rain
wipers
wave
like a tired
pair of arms
a car
makes an
emergency
stop
a homeless
man
moves
like a saw
into traffic

when
will
you
see her
again
I ask

soon

soon

now

traffic

builds

the other way

would have

been quicker

he says

to our right

a van

pulls up

two men

motion

to lower

windows

in rain

he does

we do

go home

home

go home

home

laughing
up
a storm
front
then
speeding
off

he tucks
his daughter
back in
her mother
himself
gripping
the wheel
like a
gun
how much
can a
pair of hands
keep
one of two
phones

rings
declining
the call
the song
on the radio
ends
an ad
suggests
a weekend
break to Europe
turning it
off
bringing
us right
into
where
we were
asking
what about you
do you have
children
do you prefer
it
here
?

A Line of Simple Inquiry

follows in the traditional vein of questioning when one encounters a person or persons they perceive to be other. The famous public autopsy, at a dinner party, art gallery, gymnasium or local bakery. Three words light as a baby's finger. But where *really*? The taxonomy of difference, along with the need or entitlement to ask so politely, with one hand resting on the elbow, displaying caution, not wanting to infer, with emphasis on *assume*, as in to avoid causing offence, becoming more scrutinized, every feature up against the light, your body under their knife, the question again, so as to deduce, so as to allow the remarkable recalling of definitive histories, Ibn Khaldun, Mansa Musa, Phillis Wheatley & Al Afghani, your people, as in extraordinary, as in don't take this the wrong way, as in don't take this to heart, but it's all so fascinating, an appreciation if you will, to announce so subtly, without hubris, the panoply of books read, on the way we eat & live & love & bury our dead,

& really it's all just so *interesting*, as if interest were a desperate thing scurrying across a mass grave, an artefact snatched from an old warrior's hand, neat wall text in a city museum, to cast iron eyes over, incredulity, you don't look like, the aquiline nose was the giveaway, skin thicker than animal sex that never cracks under god. All those nuances bloating the unfished ghosts of the sea, & all that hair, is that natural? Is that yours? Is it real? To touch what I own. Take what I see. There's a reason why my daddy told me to keep a stone between my fists when I fight & really it's all too complicated & everything's already been said much better by people who had it much worse, but look, is this your attempt to bid me farewell in my tongue? Are you here to help carry the burden of my name? Are your hands strong enough to lug it? We all know the stuck fishbone never meant any harm. Is that your hand still on my elbow?

Things Already Lost

A dead rat could be a dead lung
except nobody wants to touch
a dead rat without gloves.

        At the end of the funeral
        my son asks when will she
        climb out of the box.

He learnt to say 'pigeon'
by asking what the flattened
thing was in the driveway.

        Each morning for a week
        he'd run to the window waving
        at its disintegrating wings.

Like this he learnt the perils
of grapes, to grip banisters
& stand still for sun block.

In the park he insists we race
& like any good father
I make my body age.

He leaps claiming victory
I feign a sadness offering
his rapture a little more time.

He wants to keep a leaf for a pet
I want to warn him about getting
attached to things already lost.

In the bath he needs to know
where water ends when it
disappears along with dirt.

At the table he folds a napkin
into a frail boat, pushes it along
an edge.

We watch a snail work the earth
he asks if the trail is a thing
it makes or it leaves.

Ladybird blood is a firm yellow
containing only signal released
when danger's close.

He balances a blueberry
on a spoon reaching for
my hand before crossing

when a motorcyclist is down
most of us will stand one of us kneels
nobody's sure where to touch.

After the Formalities

In 1481 the word 'race' first appears in Jacques de Bréze's
poem 'The Hunt'. De Bréze uses the word to distinguish
between different groups of dogs.

In that hard year grandparents arrived on a boat
with a war behind them and a set of dog leads.
Bullet holes in the sofa. Burst pillows. Split rabbits.
Passports bound in fresh newspapers. Bomber planes.
A dissenting priest. A moneybag sucking worry.
On the boat grandmother anticipated England's
winters with the others. Slick snow on gold streets.
Grandfather grieved two dogs he'd left. Pedigrees.
Bluebottles decaying at the base of their bowls. The dogs
of England were different. The water though. Fine to drink.

In 1606 French diplomat Jean Nicot added the word 'race'
to the dictionary to denote distinctions between different
groups of people. Nicotine is named after him.

In London grandparents lived with only a radio.
A lamp favouring the wall's best side. Curtains drawn.

Byzantine icons placed on paraffin heaters.
Arguing through whispers. Not wanting to expose tongues.
Stories circulating. What neighbours do if they catch you saying
'I'm afraid' in a language that sounds like charred furniture
being dragged across a copper floor. Grandfather. Always.
Blew smoke out the lip of his window. So too did his neighbour.
Colourless plumes merging. How it's impossible to discern
the brand of cigarette a single pile of ash derives from.

> *In his 1684 essay 'A New Division of the Earth', French*
> *physician François Bernier became the first popular classifier*
> *to separate humans into races using phenotypic characteristics.*

Mother's skin is the colour of vacations.
Her hair bare-foot black. An island's only runway.
Reports of racist attacks. Father turns up the volume.
Turns us down. Chews his pork. Stings the taste with beer.
Tells mother to pass the pepper. There is never a please.
He asks if she remembers the attack. The hospital. His nose.
A Coca-Cola bottle picked from his skull. Yes. She mutters.
The chase. Dirty bitch. How we'll make you white.
Aphrodite hard. Dirty dog trembling with the street light.
Please god. Not tonight. The kids.

In his essay of 1775, 'On the Natural Variety of Mankind',
J.F. Blumenbach claimed that it was environment which
caused variety in humans.

In the bathroom mirror I spat blood from my mouth.
Quaver breath. Suburban. My brother desperate to piss.
Pulled the door open. Asking. What happened?
I tried to fight & lost. Why? Because the island
we come from is smaller than this. Their names are shorter.
Pronounceable so they exist. Even after their noses break
they still don't hook like ours. Their sun is only half-peeled.
He lifted his top to show me two bruises. To remind me
of something. How history found its own way of surviving.
A dark wash mixed with the whites spinning around & around.

In the bathroom mirror my brother spat blood
from his mouth. *Souvla* breath & home. Me.
Desperate to piss. Pulling the door open. Asking.
What happened? He tried to fight & lost. Why?
Because the island we come from is larger than this.
Here. We chew up too much of their language.
Leave behind an alphabet of bones. We will never exist
in their love songs. How many bruises does it take

to make a single body? I left him. Surviving history.
A dark wash mixed with the whites spinning around & around.

In 1859 British naturalist Charles Darwin wrote On the
Origin of Species by Means of Natural Selection, or the
Preservation of Favoured Races in the Struggle for Life.

If the house phone rings after midnight
someone you know is dying. Breathing in ten black moons
under a siren or belfry. From the wound in my uncle's back
leaked the first atlas. Blood escaping him
like a phantom vaulting over the spiked gates of heaven.
The knife. Half steel half drunk. The motive. Skin or prayer.
We went to visit. In the window's condensation his daughter
wrote, *daddy don't die.* On the water of her breath.
That evening my father came home. One hand trumpet.
The other wreath. All his fists the law.

In his seminal book of 1911, Heredity in Relation to
Eugenics, *eugenicist Charles Davenport wrote, 'Two imbecile
parents, whether related or not, have only imbecile offspring.'*

She had the same colour hair as Jesus. Most boys smile
after. When we were done I moved a blonde streak
from my arm. Wondering how much of my body

was still mine. I smelt of rain on an old umbrella.
My fingers a burnt factory. She asked if she was my first
& when I said yes she smiled. Pulling the covers up
whispering not to get too comfortable. How her father
would be back. The bed a wet flag. The duvet
breaking news. On the shelf a gollywog
above her family portrait. Poised like a saint.

The Bengal famine of 1943 killed four million people.
Churchill ordered food to be sent directly to British soldiers
in Europe. On hearing the number of Bengalis who had
perished, he asked, "why hasn't Gandhi died yet?"

Outside the KFC racists have always looked
so sure to me. Like weathermen.
Driving his skull into mine like a belief. I saw
how even evil can feel warm & smell good
when close enough. A crowbar. Wedged against
my throat. Slowly the lights began to wave. Chips
by my feet. Black iron warming my skin so silently
I could hear how suffering learns to soothe the jaws
of antiquity. These men. Irrational as any god. & me.
Emptying inside the promise of my oxygen tank.

"Those whom the gods wish to destroy, they first make mad.
We must be mad, literally mad, as a nation to be permitting
the annual inflow of some 50,000 dependants, who are
for the most part the material of the future growth of the
immigrant-descended population." — Enoch Powell, 1968.

After the formalities of course I said London
& of course he asked again. When I said Cyprus
he leaned into his chair recalling a family holiday.
The weather sublime. The people accommodating.
Particularly towards the English. How it was a shame
about the Turkish thing. & your parents. When did they enter
here? In the late '50s I replied. So before the Immigrants Act?
Yes I said. Before. Well good for them. He said.
Putting the lid on his pen. Closing his pad.
Asking me to talk a bit more about my previous roles.

In 2001 philosopher Robert Bernasconi wrote, 'The
construct of race was a way for white people to define those
who they regarded as other.'

In those days I was required to fill out forms
with multiple boxes. Some I left blank. My father
would notice my omission. Filling in the white
option with his black biro. I crossed it out.

Telling him I'm going with 'other'. My mother
wearing the same sad skin as before said we are not
white. The look he gave her was. Snatching the form
from me. The same X dominating so much white.
Let me tell you. Nobody in their right mind need
make themselves such an obvious target. He affirmed.

"It's amazing how ideas start out, isn't it?"— *Nigel Farage, 2016.*

My grandmother will die. Somewhere in her skeleton.
White sheeted. Iodoform thick. Her mouth all beetle.
My family will gather around her body. All fig. My mother
will look for coins. Despite there being nothing for money
to save. Another lady. Dying the same. Will goad our kind.
Through thick tubes she'll scorn. Her voice. A bluebottle's
hot wings. You're all dogs. Foreigners. & dirty. Outnumber us
even in dying. The nurse will apologise for the whole of history.
Drawing the curtain. Mud is always the last thing to be thrown.
A prayer reaching for the pride of an olive. Like a hint. To hold.

How Men Will Remember Their Fathers

As protagonists encumbered by their role,
chain smoking the innards of a living room parish,
decades spent with arms crossed, rejecting fragility,
lifting pints up to their confessional box.

Before we were men we would study the slopes
of shattered furniture, heed how the commands
of our fathers would curdle with a cruel logic.
We were boys then, standing beneath them as detritus,

picking from their petulance ways to parrot their alpha,
vituperative chessmen with only grey slippers on,
dreading another staircase war drum; the generals
we were unable to know because of their shell-shocked

Jesus. Father, I can fit my childhood into a fist.
I can name the times I stayed silent when you
thundered there were only two types of people,
winners and losers, forgetting the belt, the shoe,

the eyewitness.

Once I Had an Acceptance Speech

Driving too close to the kerb. Admit
to being poor. Stash pumpkin seeds
for my kid. Hustle the Christian way.
Starch my shirt collars. Value a strong
smudge. Give pigeons saintly names.
Cream both my feet. Recycle. Sign off
emails with *Warm regards*. Double tap
#vegan. Heart statuses which start with
I'm delighted to announce. Mornings.
I struggle to decide what mood to wear.
Evenings. I lie beside my aftershaves,
imagining the sea. I should really have
it by now. A Dyson. Panasonic bread-
maker. A photo by the piano of a slum
tour. I need the spirit of a full-moon party
rather than the charisma of a shed. They
honk when I slow. I swear with my eyes.
Think of real blood. Sunday comes. Dad
asks what's the plan. I knit him the only

winning scratch card. I leave a candle on
for destiny. Once. I had an acceptance
speech written. Soon. A staircase will rise
to defeat us all. The roads have moved.
When I get in I'll sit in the shower & say
it's a bath. Double-tap an ultrasound pic.
Sip railroad water. Notification. *ZANC1*
started following you. Check my speed.
Slap on another Barry Manilow playlist.
Keep my greys in the dashboard. Wonder.
What the guy who put a gun to my little
brother's head is doing for New Year's.
Wonder. If my neighbour made it through.
Up ahead. A badger's hit beside a boulder.
Its glare a wooden egg I slow for.

Oiling Brakes

'We are suffering seven directions at once' — C.K. WILLIAMS

You say I shouldn't visit / wait for the meds to kick in /
how it's all ox bullocks knocking around a poacher's sack /

you say I sound happier / I listen to the ways you breathe /
a beanbag kicked around by drunks in June /

you ask if it's raining / I say the ocean holds four out of five
living things / you take another drag / exhale scaffolding /

your voice snake skin / I ask if you need me to bring anything /
you say only the best bits / how everyone sleeps

trapped inside someone they can't stand /
how your mate made a rope by herself / for her neck /

how nobody knew how / clever bastard / who was sick
of seeing herself drooling through therapy /

three thousand hooved feet rushing over a tunnel /
a voice calling for you to finish / you say quick /

give me one more to think about / I say more than half
the British public believe in life after death /

inhaling crows / you wait before saying /
what a bunch of nutters / why bother with facts /

how our conversation's recorded / the voice again
calling / only this time you're gone //

The picture I keep of you has aged / us oiling brakes / you
peddling up a hill / storming down / palms to the sky

needing nothing / saying when a body drowns / water
compresses gasses in the chest / exploding the heart /

who told you that / and you laugh / holding my head
underwater / blood thumping against its first symptom /

the cry of a young bird on the bank / fallen from its nest /
you / lifting its suffering up to your mouth like a tonic /

its body secular / lighter than a wound in a painting / go on /
name it / but I couldn't / you / hurling it far into the brambles /

racing up the next hill / a puncture / before the fall /
breaks / screeching / at the foot of my ears / to stop

Cocaine God

you remember how it went
at the Christmas party —

I felt so man when she asked me to dance

keeping her close like the papers
I'd bring you

our bodies steady   releasing into music
hard loafers red-faced & my girl so make-believe

me dancing like that   so feline
so vague   the largeness of a man
the smallness of a boy

what was it guiding us then?
a thirst   a sorrow   the world?

you directing mum   so yes   so river

provoking her feet into space
water pulled   how kitchen is the dance?
how bedroom can it get?   her look
exultant   your expression
the latest technology owning the floor
heavy smoke   disco ball for your dips
perfume skidding on breath   eyes here
then there   you watching how I stirred
my girl   your son so deer   so calf   my dad
made of headlight pure petroleum another powder
the history of your head   rocking mine
head-butting me clean   brick on butter

the way I went   spinach leaf on steam
picking pink from off the floor   & why
her moisturised knee   the holy hills of her dress
crouching   sequins guiding me to my feet
double-eyed   with music   throbbing

& you dad   grinning like a bucket's handle
breathing in your body   bullying what endured
your tiny feet tighter than a boxer's lace
        & mum moving less like water now

more like tar

    at the table my girl handed me a beer
as if it were the end of an agonising crossword
while the rest of us watched you force yourself
into each song
    returning the years   the light
bursting through us all   black
    as the smoke of burning swans

Testimony as Omission

firstly / when the knife was put to the other man's throat /
I became elsewhere / the fourth holy city / I heard the sea's
muddy flutes lobbying tomorrow / heaving a hymn for the
things it was powerless to reach / cities it was unable to salt /
one set of eyes plunged into the other / looking to see what
could be had / there's a kind of shaking the living perform /
when the seconds that follow / all contain a dry fish / damp
incense / a figurine of a skeletal Buddha / a scratched moon

secondly / I was still a boy then / no hair to shave around
/ a mouth which didn't know how to street spit / my lungs
felt / the large nerve of a man / crack like dry saliva on a
licked cheek / and yes / I should have intervened / gazelle-
like / between two injured leopards / but there comes a
point where you realise / the worst has already happened /
only not to you / I saw the edge of the knife ride the dark of
his body / so going / I was thinking in eulogy / mumbling
a sequence of termites

I wanted to help / crayon king heckled by ballast / facing the grave's symmetry / and what words does a crazed man / give the ear to keep / seconds before the knife enters / concluding the body / where / quiet as a compass-needle / dizzying each sea symbol / he dies with the newly dead / zipping up / closing down / around a poppy field of proverbs

finally / you must understand / before I ran / blood was yet to be seen / life was still trying to worm its way home in its lowest gear / I suppose / fog gradually / ending the moth's paroxysm / and I / the only witness / caught the white of his ankles / his eyes / the whole front row / hands spoilt / and unsteady / reaching to rinse themselves in my promise

There Are No Ends, Only Intervals

'Our parents were our first colonisers' — GOENAWAN MOHAMAD

then once those white boys were done with me
they turned their god onto Francis Uwagboe
pulling the sky from under him the salmon of fists
the faith of feet curving him into another dramatic
pause his breathing mirroring a faulty generator
his pupils two slammed priests my poor Francis
who would always clock the more difficult levels
who always managed to beat the bosses in silence
was left in the hush of the forensic team's brush
the police incredulous a voice safe in its transceiver

poet Abu Dulama wrote for the first Abbasid caliph
we are alike in colour our faces are black and ugly
our names are shameful even now everything can
feel like the spine of an aged wrestler back home
we both drizzle what's left of Jesus over our cuts
what good is a crucifix if it hasn't felt anything

since being nailed to a wall today we were alive
enough to be remembered by the same white boys
who in class had no answer when asked why *Civil
Rights* was a significant turning point in history

§

then at the table Chloe's father asked me to join
for dinner I was in fact hungry but said I'd eaten
my mother raised us to act full when confronted
with a charity we couldn't trust in the garden
she said I struggled with intimacy as her father
brought secateurs up to deadhead a hydrangea
he's new to this she said its body falling like a flyer
through the door later I knelt the way a *converso*
might so as not to be seen restoring bloom to stem
with all the worry of a target

America is named after Amerigo Vespucci
a coloniser who would prove Columbus wrong
history is all of our making I wanted to declare
she said enough for one night sometimes
the only way to speak to a person who hurts

is to kiss them enough their mouth learns
how to salvage love from spit on the floor
she rolled cigarettes she was still learning
tying back her hair to unbutton the world
with a lighter in hand she called me to bed

§

then later my father hit me just a little too hard
for smoking I stayed off school reading up on
Gonçalves which proved the start of something
serious after he would declare how he loved me
and I'd ask then what would he do if he hated me
history says Gonçalves owes his lot to the Ashantis
& Dahomeys my father the logician hit me too hard
his eyes two charged weevils his willingness canine
knuckles of expired milk the door locked my mother
away on her knees begging his rage to keep me alive

then once the wedding was over Francis held his wife
the way we would our towels after a winter
by the outdoor pool later I sat with my father drinking
beer in his garden adorned by flowers we'd never seen

the quicker they grew the more they were ignored I saw
a mouse lying half-eaten beside some dog shit which
glistened symbolising relief in the middle of childhood
while on the shed a cat I thought had died long ago sat
licking its wound or listening or waiting or watching
before it leapt

Connatural

Because what can be more lonely
than a window? Elements eventually
blotting what it sees. Rain falls orphaned
and volatile. Each drop undressing itself coyly
to reveal half sea

                        half dust.

Is snow not just water that changed its mind?
Wishing instead to die cold rather than wet.
Fluid. Like us. Where we fall is where we end.
If earth is the sky's boneyard haven't we all died
before? The strong probably dying double.

                        Are muscles not just tombs
                        the strong bury tragedies in?

When the weather is warm we open windows.
Fanning our anxieties with air. Inside our homes

we arrange flowers picked carefully for their colours'
mouthless beauty. Condemned to perish upright
inside the puddled prison of a vase.

        Bats are the only mammals that can fly.
        Bats are really gods that survived.
        Only the females bite.

A painting of a hibernation cave amidst
a lightning storm is outstripped by its frame.
Its owner is a taxidermist with a penchant
for red meat and Nietzschean philosophy.
Hole in the sky. Hole in the shoe.

        Doesn't the mood around the slaughterhouse
        feel like a mugger's blade dropped into
        a baby's cot? Everything smacks
        of the colour yellow burning.

A westerly wind picks up to whip the dust
from the bookshelf. The window stands
guard. Where is everyone? Where are we all?
Locked in our cities. Drumming armless in Lycra.
Notice how we mistake night for tomorrow

looking for something pretty to wear.
Are we not sick of seeing ourselves dressed
by the same dark? The same definite voice
crawling through windows like a thief
only to discover the same silent trembling.

Saying

I know with you the room is clean   morning onwards into
     always
inside me   there are woods I want to torch   I do but don't
     and   don't
know why   so much backwater   nervous hatchet   some
     afternoons
you're the towering hour   the way you work up day   write sky in
how you do it all   without pageantry   or demand
     !   I'm doing it again   trying to say   confess
     I don't mean to push out my hurt   my split   it's just
I find this very difficult   like most truths   I've become expert in
     ruining
     I'm not sure if beatitude is a word   or why anyone would
need to say it

     after dinner   while washing I say tonight you will hold her accept one day   as will you   both done

    so I prepare   reminding myself you climb into bed

creams outfit sleep   pyjama meadows I want to say something soft

        the bold of your lashes   our son so us

sirens slap   outside on the back a burning perhaps you ask if I've

    set the alarm

                    touching light

    into off   yesterday pleats today   my mouth

a blunt axe   hunting   this exhaust   dragging   these woods.

Sublimation

beyond the first door she lays looped
around two beams of light, beneath the city
cork-bones rattle the troubled

after dark he paces the road, rewiring
half of each hour, yelling Aisha upwards,
his beard a full cloud punching air

perhaps grief is our way of keeping the dead
to ourselves, perhaps I should consider
relocating, my therapist suggested

when I asked what he thought of home
my right leg unable to still itself
a Baldwin quote at the ready

my grandmother has forgotten my name
looking wild around my face as if it's a case
housing some famous fossil in a museum

I'm unable to hold my mother's breaking,
I find a corner where I cradle my phone
furiously tapping on any photo showing teeth

my son couldn't stop thanking me for buying him
a watch, *I love you daddy*, at this I cried
becoming another rescued animal in his hands

Sympathy for Rain

Only a flood will be keen to want more
cities run you into their concrete cage
umbrellas fatten to confirm your   waste
roof tiles keep you only for your slickness
spectacles bury you   in a tissue's
neat secret   leather jokes at your attempt
little refugees of somewhere cloud   camped
in stained-glass windows what thug-grey did this
even when you soak through cloth to beg skin
you're shaken off   left to dry into loss
a slant of earth still motions your   saving
a slug slow as a monk carries you   up
asking red to soften around your name
until you are nowhere   but there   again.

Life Insurance

I shake where no hand comes to steady me. Nothing to
become. I can't be polite to chuggers anymore. Keeping it all
inside me like a map. The mole on the back of my neck has
grown another hair. Around the house, plants endure, dry
as croissants. Limescale around the faucet like a robe. I try
making myself up. Try taking the dirty nappies out. Wiping
down the condiment shelf. Descaling the kettle. Diver with
meconium on the lungs. The dog upstairs paces the floor like
it's forgotten its great routine.

You've been up all night. Between his crying, the sirens and
the other side of work I feel impossible. It's nearly next week
and he's still on. In hospital you lay beside him as if you leased
the insides of a runaway yellow. The worst thing about life is
how suffering outlives us. There's not much you wish to give
anything to & I feel underwhelming, a sandbag. In the car
I broke down at the end of a radio ad. Something about life
insurance. A parking attendant taps on the window pointing
to his watch. For the next two miles I jump every red light.

A Boy Stood Still

With the tip of my elbow dipped in, I float the yellow duck to be sure. 37° flashes a solid green. The story goes, my uncle made his son sit in a bathtub of ice water for half an hour. The boy's teeth chattering at such a rate they say they nearly ruptured his mouth. The water around your belly unlocks. Opening. Your body still dubious until it trusts; looking back, the punishment itself never appalled me, more the thought of what a father decides to do with himself during the time his ten-year-old son is sat in a tub of ice water. Aside from check his watch & wait.

I'm your father & the only person keeping you alive. In the mirror I trace your name until both our faces burst out the other side. You will have no memory of this. At the end of every Bruce Lee film my cousins and I would claim a character. Re-enacting the most epic scene. Fantasy finding a way to travel up & towards. Michael forced a cushion over my face long enough. His laugh. When I came back round my uncle had a hand around his throat. Dragging him to the bathroom. Ice cubes rattling like milk teeth inside a tank's hatch. A turn.

Patricide

This morning we're reading your favourite book, starting at the end. I was ten when I almost killed my father. Releasing the handbrake. Watching the truck roll. You're old enough to end sentences. Grappling with the faith of gist. He was in the toilet. His friends joked: *holy shit.* I expected him to come out crawling. His heart caught between his ribs like a fawn trapped among the rails. He lit a cigarette. Repositioned his tie. Exhaling a few bloodshot thorns. Wrapping myself around his waist, I whimpered. Drool softening the edges of his belt. Four knuckles pacifying me. A sharp kick to an old dog's gut.

Tonight I'll read you another bedtime story about something absurd & you'll find a way to dream the feelings. Across the Milky Way an alien boy is sat by the sidewalk scavenging his father's shadow for a gift. One day he'll have to watch him die & forge shelter from a memory. What life will do to us in the name of living. Why do all children's stories rely so heavily on falsity? Isn't astrology a pseudoscience? My boy, your breathing has abated to the pace of letter writing. With a single pull of the blinds I can either kill the moon or teach you the night.

Nautical Almanac

Let me show you the ocean. In the car you sleep through the songs I play. Someday I'll explain. How we take such vague steps into our years leaving chunks of what tried to end us everywhere. Love doesn't believe in dying a good death. I have forgiven my inventions. At least the water here is honest enough to be cold. Testing tomorrow with our toes. The swoop of a scared bird can make us all seem inadequate. Science says the universe wants only to begin. We're the only species who understand we will one day die. For now, nothing wants to know more.

On board the ferry I lift you high onto my shoulders. Both of us facing tomorrow. Fatherhood can be summed up this way. In my mind you're searching & I'm your nautical almanac. *Daddy, do birds ever wear out the view? How does a root cross a curled worm? Do you think ants get lonely? Which moon does history own? Why do some people die with their heads bent down? Why are your eyes doing that? Who is the man in the photo? Will you be my daddy forever?* It's impossible to really answer anything with this much spray. This much sickness. If I were to jump in the ocean, would you remember?

Talking to Myself in Halves

you will ask

        wanting the tunnel to explain
        its darkness

needing the answer
to be more than echo

Meeting the End of the World as Yourself

Plasters come off under water

hardly anyone gets to die
the way they want

rain only ever looks good
from the inside —

       sit up
you sound like a defamed fact

most men die before they reach
seventy-seven

you've always been too small a miracle

rub these blades
wait to hear the executioner's

whistle before you panic

mosquitos have been doing this
for much longer than you
and they look great

your mother lied

certain people
will never want to pronounce you

whoever told you
this was a good idea?

you ever kissed
a mnemonist in your sleep?

name two people
who'll die for you;

how long have you wanted this?

these eyes of adoration

this whole new side.

shall I tell you
what I think?

you look like cholesterol.

in the 1920s
people believed smoking
was good for them

what's a mistake but anathema
waiting for science.

show me your hands
turn them round

use them to dig
or punch or stay
but don't tell me
you really thought these
are what spoke to god

I've had toothbrushes
more complicated than you
you look like a social construct
on the scrap heap of history

you know why she left
why he never picked up
because the world is on fire
and the same thing can never burn twice

but in all honesty, I wouldn't worry

fill your bellybutton with the ashes
of your neighbour's dog
the one who died of cancer

you were only born
to make the colour grey look good.

quickly,
when was the last time
you gargled magnets?

what year was your mother born?

what will you leave behind
when you force oblivion
to take you?

there's violence in forgetting

never confuse your head
        for memory

I've told the coroner to expect you
                in the morning

whatever refuses to stop
                        fails to survive

What the Lesser Water Boatman Had to Say

Think of a space where light folds into a hem
                now suppose movement
algae nesting buoyancy   quiet as underneath
callow   away from human sides

a past so dense   which happened   only to us
I wish to know things   other than ghosts
    endlessly   translating water   into sound
insecta pond prisoner   to be here is to be there

but you with your symbols golf courses drinks
cabinets   bring us down   what is it you want?
Skin tone overseers   manic brutes   bullet hungry
& burning   where did you rehearse?

I ruminate on those returned before arrival
    finished   by a spit-born weapon   once
I spoke against darkness my punishment to be shunned

with the backswimmers & plankton

we pick cartilage from the ribs of our sorrows
we   the unheard of   struck
the opposite of wheat   how the smallest things
     learn the conceit of a microscope's lens

the cold of the Mariana Trench   a fisherman's regret
what do you know about me?   My name a second face
a spell of mirrors   old hands wiping the body down
what have you seen born?   What have you seen die?

The rain's duped the Astro Turf again   the end
lives inside   everything   still you assume
I swim backwards   towards my loss   when
I move forwards   towards my tide   title: Lesser

subject of the Metazoa who sings from the spot
     for the strange storms   lusting flotillas
the black   running
     translating water   into sound

Jeremy Corbyn at the Doctor's Surgery

On my 35th birthday I lay dying. Returning to the doctors
to learn what my chances were. Among the sick I waited.
Coughs. Sneezes. Croaks. Three boys bickering over toys.
The exact same ones I remember seeing as a kid.

My father says *anything too loud is probably lying*. I picked up
a paper and tried hard not to listen. Tossed gum into my mouth.
Then he walked in. The whole surgery disbelieving. Soundless.
He pulled a tissue from his pocket. Then blew his nose.

A painter had spent his whole life trying to master the sky.
When he died his daughter taped his last watercolour to the inside
of his coffin. Forfeiting the eulogy. But this was worse.
We needed proof. The lady beside me stopped drafting her email.

The elderly couple stopped rummaging for lottery tickets.
The receptionist crunched down on her boiled sweet. Even the kids
forgot their wars. While he just sat there. Basic as a tent.
Twisting a tissue. Waiting. Like the rest.

A man with a face like a glove. Walked in. Both eyes
sodden beer mats. His dog. Rhapsodic in its boxed frame
came scuttling behind. Sniffing him out. Licking his shoes.
As if somehow it knew the reason dogs were allowed in.

I explained to the doctor. Again. How my problems
started around 2016. And how Jeremy Corbyn was, in fact,
sat outside waiting to be seen. Removing his spectacles.
Exhaling. He asks, "really, are you not exhausted by all of this yet?"

Separation Has Its Own Economy

having fallen through the mirror in my chest, having become
my tardiest wound, I decided to invent a new me although
some things are practically impossible like trying to hurry
haze, or forcing colour onto blue; I press my cheeks onto
hot bulbs, move furniture into who cares, knock on doors
with my gums, finger phone boxes for forgotten change.

My habits consist of dialling the wrong number just to hear
myself say I'm sorry, crushing the stems of daffodils into
Ikea mugs we bought in a Dalston charity shop; each night
when the emails stop, I go on eBay to bid £306 on a key
shaped bottle opener, three MDF penguins and a soft toy
with cigarette burns. Nobody outbids me.

Things I keep because I must:
> a court summons for two unpaid parking tickets
> a tattoo of your PIN on my wrist.

For the past month I've been ripping the heads off fishes
giving each a sobriquet before French-kissing their dead eyes.

All that remains:
        a Jamie Oliver cook book,
        a date circled in red for a beginner's salsa class,
        organic wine I was sent after a talk
                on gentrification in east London.

Up for grabs is a discounted meal for two and tweezers too
    small for my hands:

On better days I envisage myself a man
who owns a house in Zone 4 with a garden,
casually mowing the lawn in early spring
the way a secular thinker might.

For the occasion I'd wear tight white shorts
combined with a salmon pink sweater
my Chihuahua named Nico
will keep tangling himself up in the lead.

On the patio will be an Aperol Spritz half
savoured while through the double glazing
my wife will be reading *Capital* to our children,
all eight of them, at exactly the same time.

This is what I envision as I saunter to Dan's flat
unfurnished and smelling of attempt.

There I ask to borrow his saw, a hammer, a rope. He tells
me to behave. I say some things are in need of fixing. He
sits me down. Says his girlfriend only got with him because
she didn't want her kids to come out too pasty. Said she told
him that in a text. Said racism is its own logic. Said he told
her to go find a white guy and a two-bed above a sunbed
parlour. Said orange is the new black, anyway.

There's only so many ways you can remember a person. My
friend Dan. Who lent me a saw, a hammer but kept back
the rope, along with his sense of humour.

Ecumene

'America is a giant. Cyprus is a flea.' — LYNDON B. JOHNSON

I've always wanted more

to point & cry & say look, but you
made yourself mock, embarrassed history.

Mates would say *where?* when everywhere
was stuck on a classroom wall, when the sea
hosting the facile gull wore you like spume

all nook & noun; when Mr Dhondy
listed Britain's ex-colonies he omitted you;
pitiable street-sweeper stalking trash,
bring me zoom, call Pluto for a giggle,

olive bruise I wished you mass or whisper
tucked into the world's waist like a crease,
why make me explain you until my mouth

became a scythe, why bifurcate — Europe
or the Middle East, myth or ganglion.

(in my room I hung you above my bed —
white for breaking yellow for copper
green for possibility your north * south
I saw you emboldened, bursting
across the Levant with a geography
all yours standing up for us. her rock.)

One afternoon Mr Dhondy asked
us to pin-mark our origins, approaching
with cartographic care, the syringed tip
almost historic, curious glances, chortles
at Pakistan Somalia Palestine India,
short empires of pinheads colonising
the board

the bodies of our belonging pockmarked
I stepped up, pin ready, stopping to seek you,
fiduciary calling, crunched between giants
like armpit hair, driving that bastard in
just to hear you say something, idle lump
announce yourself to the world, this class,

but you knew only to divide, spread wounds,
lacerations where cultures rush to babble.

Some years later I will be in San Diego
where I'll become a game for Americans
wanting to place me, your name shearing
their teeth, abstract algebra, you're still
too small to fit anything, I elucidate
as best I can, they settle for Turkey
Egypt Greece Dominican Republic —
later I'll stare at you until you're dead
& I can say yes to them all.

Moving out my parent's house at thirty
I put you in a box with East 17 cassettes,
Swiss army knives & souvenir lighters,
by then I'd stopped bothering, accepted
what I must, knowing you at least cart sun
& the young still look to party with you;
we took time when considering the walls,
where best to hang things, what we wanted
seen, applauded, by the hundreds of visitors
we eventually invited in.

Following on from Kant

'The business of philosophy is not to give rules, but to analyse the private judgments of common reason' — IMMANUEL KANT

> *The Negros of Africa have, by nature, no feeling*
> *that rises above the trifling*

The Hermetica's spine blunt with forgetting
twists race into a white noose poor Siculus who assumed
from Heliopolis to Königsberg it was clear who the autochthones were

> *Mr. Hume challenges anyone to cite a single*
> *example in which the Negro has shown talents*

~~Sun-god~~ ~~Pyramids~~ ~~Mauretania~~ ~~Nok~~ ~~Igbo-Ukwu~~
Ra   Meroe Kush   Moors   Nigera   Bronzes

> *and asserts that among the hundreds of thousands*
> *of blacks who are transported elsewhere from their*
> *countries*

~~House of Wisdom~~   Songhai   Steam Engines   ~~Water Clock~~
~~Thermometer~~   Fatimid Caliphs   ~~Mali~~   ~~Heron~~   Egypt   ~~Egypt~~

although many of them have been set free still not
a single one of them was found who presented
anything greater

Mathematics   Algorithm   Astronomy   Physics   Medicine
Algebra   ~~al-Khwārizmī~~   ~~Ibn Yunus~~   ~~Alhazen~~   ~~Al-Zahrawi~~

in art or science or any other praise worthy quality

Music   Poetry   Painting
~~Chevalier de Saint-Georges~~ ~~Phillis Wheatley~~ ~~Warrick Fuller~~

even though among the whites some continually
rise aloft from the lowest rabble

what comes before a fact?

i asked my history teacher on the last day of lessons. who instead of answering insisted i try identifying the last of the boys. my lips goose fat. my posture a paper clip. those boys whose hands were at home taking apart bodies like mine. my name limp between their jaws. a crunch. he knew that. saying it was learnt behaviour. pushing the photo closer of the Asian lad they'd struck. how they beat the future from his eyes. my teacher's voice a cheap wig asking me again to try. but all i wanted was to kick a ball against a black sun and win for once. before.

in year seven. the last boy's mother walked me home. stopping first at his house where in the living room hung a Union Jack just above *the critique of pure reason*. a pair of boots below. history taking its time to turn both blonde. his dad fixed roofs for a wage. us. the same little age outside kicking a ball against the fence. his father returning home. his whistle suddenly stuck. seeing the two of us like that. practising. i mean. we can't really be made to bleed this way. from all that before. from such distance. but we can.

and through superior gifts earn respect in the world

our enemies spit empires   name comets & diseases

their footnotes   rotten chromosomes

        Locke – Buffon – Hume – Gobineau
        Darwin – Haeckel – Grant – Galton
        Hitler – Leopold

oracular speakers sure as the white in snooker balls
    governing baize

        knocking blood which is also knocking bodies
        a hangover of violence sure as the black ball

being struck. & pushed. & prodded. & poked.
    so as to finally sink which is also to triumph & end

        our enemies are here & not here
        detesting meat eaters or those wearing fur

applauding children when they die
    waking up early to water their plants

        so fundamental is the difference between these two
        races of man

in a white field stands a white man in a white shirt questioning a white god while his white dog chases a white rabbit into a black hole. its head wedged between blackness. absent solstice. extreme with bad history. the rabbit races past white millionaires sipping sunlit champagne at such a terrible time. races past the flotilla of a John Hawkins whose sails lash to capture ancient atrocities. hunched philosophers thumbing through the whites of their texts. the blacks of their Bibles. looking for a reason to curse the curse of white rabbits. running from black dogs whose heads are still wedged between the whiteness of a hole. past burning ships past burning fruit past villages and libraries and towers engulfed by greed. a Baptist minister from Atlanta a socialist from the Eastern Cape a democratically elected leader contained by the black of his jail. the white of his fate. a Franz Boas throwing a rope up to the screaming century. the black hole widening - stopping to become another white. the rabbit. its beating heart weak as wax. an invented burning. the dog stuck & stupid & smart & still at the start. its head a famous period on a decadent timeline. its breath of flesh rancid. commanding the pallbearers to hurry it up. the white man from back when nods then whistles hard for his dog to return. its face capped in dirt. no matter. the way it still obeys. shaking off the earth. returning its white. preparing tomorrow.

Biographer

they called to say it's a matter of days.
I've been up trying to work out where.
in the shower I cried an adult body.
like a school of dolphins coming apart.
what month is this anyway?

and why you? why now? what happens
when the thought of your life. in that way.
is she in pain? will she hurt? they say no.
does she have sunlight? I say please.
open every window in that room.

wheel her to where the light remembers.
let her lay. let her. even without seeing
be still. relief. let her climb. not fall.
nobody wants to fall. lay her head.
a kiss for her feet. prayer. let her decide.

remind her of her husband's name. his dogs.
grant her intervals. water. zephyr. a hand.
this is her. pack up the tarot cards. place ears
over her mouth. her. who bought me music.
maracas. drums. guided me towards.

now her death rattle. the sun's last treaty.
where is it? has it moved? please.
I want to retain what's left. time. smell.
pick orchards from her cheeks. round up
a few good birds. sounds from her village.

she. who taught me to write. to sip sound.
use language for closeness. for closure.
I just can't see her in that way. clinical.
when grandmothers die our first strength
disbands. who will I practise with?

correct my inflection. they've called to say
it's a matter of hours. your body steadying.
I'm thinking back to those years. in your garden.
me. standing outside your house. a door.
everything has changed. I ring the bell.

Kentish Town. 1982. you're wearing green.
I'm preparing to be born. you open the door
to nothing. a van pulling away. a lift. and close.
heading back into your garden. where you'll
sit under the sun and wait for me there.

i.m. Στεδε

Unpronounceable Circle

this is how I'm going to say it he said
your surname a newborn baby's mitt impossible
to master a needle shoved into the back foot
of light six schoolboys growing into a circle
whatever stands inside dies Bible dust
by my bedside table half of me on psalms
in red biro the teacher repeats me wrong
typewriter teeth grinning at rough baptism
a leather wasp boxing olive skin I stood
transfixed beneath a white rope wondering
if Jamal al-Din Abu'l-Faraj ibn al-Jawzi
had the same problem how close I came
to the feet of doormen ornithophobia
trailing violent as young woodpeckers

five schoolboys growing into a circle
becoming wet horse hair the boy
who rammed me against his garden
fence hanged himself four weeks later

when I heard I buried three oil lamps
the blast he gave my ribs lives on
his mother gathered ants from outside
the earth releasing them over her dress
the blackest red I'd ever seen his brother
gripped her as she spun like a Cold War fan
all of us then that boy her son his brother
hated tomorrow left us sucking vinegar
from two grey feathers to his heaven
I came with the closing circle to name.

I Kissed a Dead Man's Mouth in May

it was like a weapon   walrus tusk

but it wasn't dead enough yet   was it uncle   remember?

   when water knelt before us   & you asked me to count the doves

you blew into the blue   that day uncle   a small boat in water

both our shadows   marooned   craving sand   breathing talcum

whole spikes in our lungs   uncle   why winter then?   why the
   throat first?

what happened to our throats?   why did May become so sad?
   the help

empty   handed   leaving ~~uncle~~   both of us   sharing ghosts

remember the boy uncle   who kissed a dead man's mouth in May

because he couldn't reach his eyes   in time   funny   how many
   apologies

fill a life   my uncle   it's been years   since I lifted your death

from out the water   black baptism   said those white words to your
   wife

dead uncle   uncle's dead   my uncle died   (~~I'm sorry~~)   he's dead

let me hold you one last time uncle   & try to get the letting go right

I can't get it wrong anymore   not this time   time   left   uncle

returning me each day   to the moment   when the sea

    made more sea from him

his eyes still open in me   & he had never died   & you have never died

not in any May   not with my mouth still on yours & perhaps   my

    my arms weren't solid enough

enough to breathe you back in   or back up   so what do I do now

    with all this May

 spinning   slipping through   your hand still in mine   your mouth

chewing its last meal   the taste of bread   I'm still tasting bread

soft as chest hair   the last sea-hole where he sunk

from there   where did you end up?   what world did you find more

    gentle than this?

I'm in the future now   uncle   with   your shirt   still in its Spring

a sandal floating towards   your body   its heart   so almost here.

i.m. C.P.

Two Daughters. Their Mother.

Her eldest leant over the bed
in an attempt to hear what
she was trying to say, again,
she pointed only towards the saints,
her breath fetid, her skin a shrinking network.

Each time they lowered her arm
    she would raise it again,
the eldest daughter whispered, 'the door',
the other sobbed 'the saints',
                both were right.

After the service her youngest stood in the room
to ask where she'd gone, was she tucked
safely into her ashes, satisfied with her death,
will she look back on this gamble she took
    at living and laugh?

Her slippers filling a basket,
mugs cleared from the cabinet top,
    the door closed
leaving those saints to ponder piety
as if they too have been instructed to wait.

A kneeling flame floats on the mercy
of its oil, quietly untying its light.
A petal of smoke remains, the saints
discarded until the next one is summoned
to point to where a candle is slowly lit.

A Discursive Meditation on the Photograph

of image and frame, holding subject
matter by its considered light, can you see,
sentences of angularity, the grammar
of buildings, uniformed neon, the emblem
of something flying, something falling,
middle-distance stare, the popinjay moves
to occupy more corners, dinky libertine,
the sky grows from out your shoulders
garlanded by the matted hair of poverty,
set the coffee on the table, road-kill aesthete,
rushing to buy a footprint in sand;
what is more necessary, the ocean's blue
or hope? Panoramic view blinded by light's lack.

A matchstick model of a church
is balanced on a child's wrist, pray or play?
Move around, hold still for me now, dead
corpse, so stunning and dead, bomb-blast

silent, exploded flash, broken footage,
all barren and ruddy, carnage of apathy,
gruesome and exposed and somehow
newsworthy, dreaming of porn, death porn,
dead porn, murder fatigue, war is a woman
trembling and nude, a man boneless,
war is a boat with a continent in tow,
a grin of bastards, move away from me,
chamomile tea calm, flower market Sundays,

dreamy and bucolic, place it properly,
change the lens, make it personal,
move around, take another antiseptic song,
blue infirmary, where days are drained
by cancer, and there are tumours in the water,
the nurses' steady lift onto the bed
is in memory of closed mortuaries
and those further afield, hold my hand
before I die and I love you, hold my hand
as I am born and I love you, a life spent asking
for help, asking for love, do you love me?
Do I look good in this body? In this red
or this green, every colour is alone;

try taking it from over there,
airbrush the moon's stretchmarks,
ask the river to pout, ask the sea to smile,
how many sunsets do we bury in ourselves
before we die and still my sadness
can be nothing but human,
flummoxed and looking to forget,
can you see, can you feel the breath

of each brick in this city, we are born
to a siren and the wail of each other,
I'll drink to that, and pray with dog shit
on my shoe and a bladder full of piss
can you   see,

    everyone gather round
my worst side,   asymmetric as rock,
this is a honeymoon calling for a rescue
boat, a penny balancing on a baby's heart,
this is me wanting to look like I've been
    painted
by someone other than   myself,
give me direction,   show me god,

keep me still, push
                    me down,
wash my   thoughts before you
     shoot,
everything is looking for release,

say you look tired,
                    talk to me about love
the people
          you remember

say something different
                    something strange

talk to me about funerals

     the men
who stand apart from their wives
     ask me to look up

say there you are

               can you see?

From Here the Camera Crew

looks like good news
from the room above
father yells
we're lucky to live in a democracy
    and I believe
the last July of an octogenarian
mourning what could never be
a sparrow delaying its lift
as if apologising to the oak tree
for having to die in the exact place
it was born.

They're sipping Old Fashioned
in their gardens tonight
deckchairs facing the sun
father yells
we're lucky to live in a democracy
    and I believe
the body of a boy in Dalston

the brightness of a screen
a police officer's hands black
as a belt   it's true
worms have learnt to dig
themselves out of the sweetest fruits.

Across the flyover a tower
crammed what hurt it knew
into a flame   politicians pick
soundbites from out their crooked teeth
squinting at the brightness of a screen
our nation a slow animal
unable to digest any more meat.

Inheritance

He returns in his overcoat, whispering time.
I fall into the drift. Moving past decades,
white fields pointing to a younger me, he asks
if I recognise the place. I'm caught by the eyes
of a stray cat, its body a sack of fear, I ask to break
but we don't, moving on towards my father
who stands waiting with his first-born. I stretch out
a hand, the boy knows only to flinch. I ask
to break but we don't, passing a mangled fox
waiting its saint. I try to sound out a warning,
my voice caught on the edge of the skyline's net.

We arrive at a room, my mother cradles my face,
her words seem jammed, he asks if I remember
what happened, if I'm to blame for his rage,
a snubbed paradigm, in the corner a man hunched,
a woman attempting, he brushes her off,
climbing into his overcoat, headed for a sign,
we're all here as shards, what time does to the face;

Why have we stopped? And why here? Like this?
He's heavy and earthbound, his overcoat
splayed across the final shame, a tyrant's lisp,
leaving me to labour these unmarked provinces.

ACKNOWLEDGMENTS

I'm immensely grateful to the editors of the following magazines who published earlier versions of these poems: 'Things Already Lost' was published in *Poetry London*; 'After the Formalities' in *The Poetry Review*; 'Once I Had an Acceptance Speech' in *POETRY*; 'Connatural' in *The Feminist Review*; 'Sublimation' in *The Rialto*; 'A Boy Stood Still' in *Wildness*; 'Ecumene' in *Oxford Poetry;* and 'A Discursive Meditation on the Photograph' and 'Unpronounceable Circle' in *Granta*.

NOTES

ORIGIN. 'Flames lambent' is taken from Enoch Powell's 'Rivers of Blood' speech which historian David Starkey quoted in a 2011 interview following the London riots.

FOUR SMALL INDISCRETIONS. The phrase 'forty sperm' was a prominent slur used by Greeks to denote Cypriots. A people they perceived as being 'mongrel like' in their genetic makeup.

UBER. This poem was written in response to an incident which took place on the day of the 2016 EU Referendum.